Welcome to our 11 Year Anniversary Issue, a double issue. We are excited to feature Jennifer Irene back on the cover of Kandy magazine. Jennifer is making her fourth Kandy cover appearance and fifth feature. We hope you enjoy our interview with Jennifer as we discuss her tactical training with celebrities. Hence, the "Shooting With The Stars" theme. Our little play on the words of the television series "Dancing With The Stars."

With the return of Fall comes the return of our favorite time of the year for sports. We are huge hockey fans at Kandy. We share our NHL Top 10 and bottom 5.

As common as the leaves changing colors in New England, Apple releasing new models of their iPhone is a September hallmark. This year's iPhone 14 Pro is the mobile phone to top all mobile phones. Apple's Fall lineup also rolls out their 2nd generation AirPod Pro and a new series of Apple watches. The Apple Watch 8 is specifically targeted toward women, and the Watch Ultra is for the active outdoorsman.

Fans of Game of Thrones or The Lord of the Rings will be pleased with the prequel series tailored to their appetite. First, House of Dragon is a fiery prequel to Game of Thrones, set 200 years earlier. Actress Milly Alcock has won our admiration for the portrayal of a young Prince Rhaenyra Targaryen. The Lord of the Rings sequel, The Rings of Power, also features a powerful female lead, Galadriel played by Morfydd Clark. Of the two series through their few few episodes, House of Dragon has been more entertaining than The Rings of Power. The Rings of Power has focused more on character development than action in the first few episodes.

We wrap up our 11 Year Anniversary featuring a collection of cover models from previous anniversary issues with Khloe, Nikki Leigh, Amanda Paris, and Tawny Jordan. We hope you enjoy this issue as much as we enjoyed compiling the articles and pictorials for you.

Enjoy.

Editor-In-Chief
Ron Kuchler

Managing Editor
David Packo

Associate Editor
Steve Scala

Marketing and Advertising
Bill Nychay

Cover Model
Jennifer Irene

Cover Photo Credits
Photographer Charles Rodriguez
Hair and Makeup Jennifer Irene
Location Monarch Beach, California

Contributors
Mario Barberio, Mike Prado,
Tony Piazza, Jenya Luzan
Jaime Morton Hawley, Teddy Field,
Mort McNamara, Jason Murphy

Contact Information
7260 W. Azure Drive Unit 140-639
Las Vegas, NV 89130

Subscriptions
subscriptions@kandymag.com

Customer Support
support@kandymag.com

Copyright
editor@kandymag.com

General Inquiries
support@kandymag.com

www.kandymag.com
instagram.com/kandymagazine
facebook.com/kandymagazine

One Stop for Everything Kandy
https://linktr.ee/kandymagazine

CONTENTS

WORDS, WORDS, WORDS

Geek Alert

The iPhone 14 Pro
They come in the color Purple. Let us repeat that. They come in the color Purple, and you will be the envy of all the ladies in your life and who cross your path.

2nd Generation AirPods Pro Cha-ching!
The H2 chip cancels up to twice as much noise over the previous generation

Apple Watch Ultra Go Ultra or Go Home
It has a new bold design and a wide range of elements built for endurance, exploration, and adventure.

Apple Watch 8 Geared to women
Apple Watch 8 features a large, Always-On Retina display and a crack-resistant front crystal and all-day 18-hour battery life.

Oh My Stream!

All Hail Televisions Dragon Queen, Princess Rhaenyra
In the realm of the House of Dragon, only one type of person may ascend to the Iron Throne, and that person must be a dragonrider.

The Rings of Power Galadriel is One Shrew Elf
Galadriel, played by Morfydd Clark, exemplifies strength and insight as she rallies elves and humans to confront the Orc army emerging in the Southlands.

Escape From Kabul
The documentary unfolds over 18 monumental days in August 2021, following the U.S. troop withdrawal from Afghanistan through the subsequent evacuation of tens of thousands of Afghan citizens

Sports Fanatics!

NHL Top 10
Last season we discovered that the teams that best execute the trading deadline will undoubtedly enjoy the best postseasons.

NHL Bottom 5 + 5 Wannabes
The bad teams are truly bad. And they make no bones about their desire to be the worst of the worst.

CONTENTS

Jennifer Irene

Shooting With The Stars

Our half Taiwanese, half Mexican, all-American cover model fires on all cylinders in her latest Kandy cover shoot and sharing insights on a few of the Hollywood celebrities she worked with at Taran Tactical.

FEATURES

NHL 2022-2023 SEASON BOTTOM 5

Let's get straight to the bottom of the issue in the NHL. The bad teams are truly bad. And they make no bones about their desire to be the worst of the worst. We were planning an examination of the ten worst. However, as we dove deep into the first five, they clearly separated themselves from the rest of the pack. And not in a good way. We decided to list, under Honorable Mention, the remaining five teams that appear unlikely to compete for playoff berths. So, who will be this season's worst five teams in the NHL?

Chicago Black Hawks
Gutted. Describe the Chicago Black Hawks offseason. The big excitement around the Black Hawks this season will be the Patrick Kane and Jonathan Toews watches. Where will each of those players choose to play? The Black Hawks have no leverage with either player in a trade. Where they land will depend on which NHL Stanley Cup contender can tamper the most with the player and his agent without getting caught. Kane's heart may want the New York Rangers, but NY's GM Drury and head coach Gallant may not have reciprocal feelings. The Kandy odds say Kane winds up in Edmonton to play alongside McDavid.

Arizona Coyotes
Laughingstock of all professional franchises. Describe the state of the Coyotes. For the next couple of NHL seasons, the Coyotes will play home games in a college arena. The Coyotes will play all their home games at the Arizona State University venue from 2022-23 through the 2024-25 NHL season, with an additional option for the 2025-26 season. The arena's capacity is 5,000. Unfortunately for the 'Yotes, even with the limited seating, they will continue to feel like a road team in home games. Arizona hockey fans are transplants, cheering for their hometown team, not the Coyotes. The NHL should face the reality that hockey is dead in the desert.

Montreal Canadiens
Heading into the 2021-2022 NHL season, the Canadiens were coming off a shocking appearance in the Stanley Cup final. Halfway through the season, they were in a team teardown and rebuild. The upcoming 2022-2023 season will be light on wins and another lottery chance at the top pick in the NHL draft. Led by Juraj Slafkovsky, the top pick in the 2022 NHL draft, the youth of Montreal will lead them back to the playoffs in the 2023-2024 season.

Philadelphia Flyers
The flyers hired John Tortorella as head coach. Torts, as he is known by fans, will light a fire under the team. He is an intense, no-nonsense head coach. Hockey fans around the league are intrigued by how he will mesh with free agent signee Tony DeAngelo. Offensively talented defenseman DeAngelo has a bad reputation in and out of the NHL.

Buffalo Sabres
Rounding out our bottom five, the Sabres may rise to the bottom six or seven. The Sabres have young talent, including defenseman Owen Power, the top pick in the 2021 NHL draft. Buffalo's management is not serious about winning this season, as validated by choosing 41-year-old Craig Anderson as their top goaltender. Perhaps, they are clinging to aspirations that Finnish goalie Ukko-Pekka Luukkonen will rise to his promise of a top goaltender.

Honorable Mention
Fans of the following teams may be teased early in the season to a potential post-season berth but should prepare for a 2023 Spring absent of NHL hockey - San Jose Sharks, Seattle Kraken, Ottawa Senators, Detroit Red Wings, and New York Islanders.

NHL 2022-2023 SEASON TOP 10

NHL TOP 10

Next month, a complete analysis of the upcoming 2022-2023 NHL season, including our pick to hoist the Stanley Cup in 2023.

Last season we discovered that the teams that best execute the trading deadline will undoubtedly enjoy the best postseasons.

GM Chris Drury of the New York Rangers mastered the trading deadline last season, adding veterans who were instrumental in the team reaching the Eastern Conference finals.

Who will be this season's Chris Drury?

Currently, this is our 2022-2023 season Top 10.

Colorado Avalanche – until dethroned, the Avs are number 1.

Boston Bruins – in a few words, new head coach Jim Montgomery.

Las Vegas Golden Knights – again, in a few words, new head coach

New York Rangers – as long as Igor is between the pipes, they are a top 5 team.

Edmonton Oilers – goaltending keeps them from being higher on the list.

Carolina Hurricanes – their offseason is underestimated immensely.

Calgary Flames – significant offseason roster shakeup but still a contender.

St. Louis Blues – solid roster with solid goaltending.

Toronto Maple Leafs – another season will come and go with no Cup in Toronto.

Florida Panthers – was last season a fluke? New Panther Matt Tkuchuzk will try to prove otherwise.

Nikki Leigh
"5 Year Anniversary Cover Model"
NIKKI'S WORLD
Military Appreciation, Cartwheels & Sunflower Seeds

Photos by Mario Barberio
Hair and Makeup Michelle Vanderhule
Stylist Joi Salvador

First off Nikki, congratulations on landing the cover of our 5-Year Anniversary issue. It seems as if we have been talking about shooting a cover for 5 years.
I can't believe it has been 5 years. I know I was in the 2013 Swimsuit Issue but I am excited to finally shoot a cover for Kandy. One thing I learned in life was patience is a virtue and I am honored to be on the 5 Year Anniversary cover.

CARTWHEELS AND HAPPINESS
As we were reviewing the photos we noticed you've got some serious biceps. What's your fitness regimen?
One thing I know about fitness is to always keep your body guessing. Don't do the same workout regimen all the time which is why I like to do sports and try new things. I was a gymnast when I was a little girl and I was always doing handstands and cartwheels. I have had these arms since I was like 5.

Do you still do handstands and cartwheels?
I'll do a cartwheel every now and then. When I feel extra happy.

Have you been able to get your workouts in while on location in Turkey?
I travel with resistance bands and occasionally I get into the hotel gym. It has been tough due to the early call times.

Nikki Salutes The USO & Our Military
Not your normal Kandy shoot. Why a tribute to the military?
OMG! When we talking about the shoot I remembered that 2016 was the 75th Anniversary of the USO, that what made we want to do this. I wanted to show military appreciation.

It is quite the tribute to the fighting men and women of our Armed Forces. You've got a B-29 bomber, a General's car from WWII, a helicopter from Vietnam, a troop carrier from the Korean war, a C-141 Starlifter from the Vietnam war, even a single-engine bi-plane from 1930. What was it like taking a trip through our 20th Century military timeline?
We had an amazing location that really stayed true to our history; fighter jets, helicopters, military vehicles and all the while learning the history of the planes and equipment. It was an educational shoot as well. It was really amazing to me we were able to around real life bomber planes and cargo planes that were used in historical events. It gave me a whole new respect for our history and meant more than just an ordinary photo shoot. Plus, I had my favorite crew with me – hair makeup, photographer and stylist.

Which aircraft was the most impressive to you?
I enjoyed the cargo plane, it had so much history and richness to me. Our consultant on location let us know that it is so big that they throw events inside it. I found that amazing.

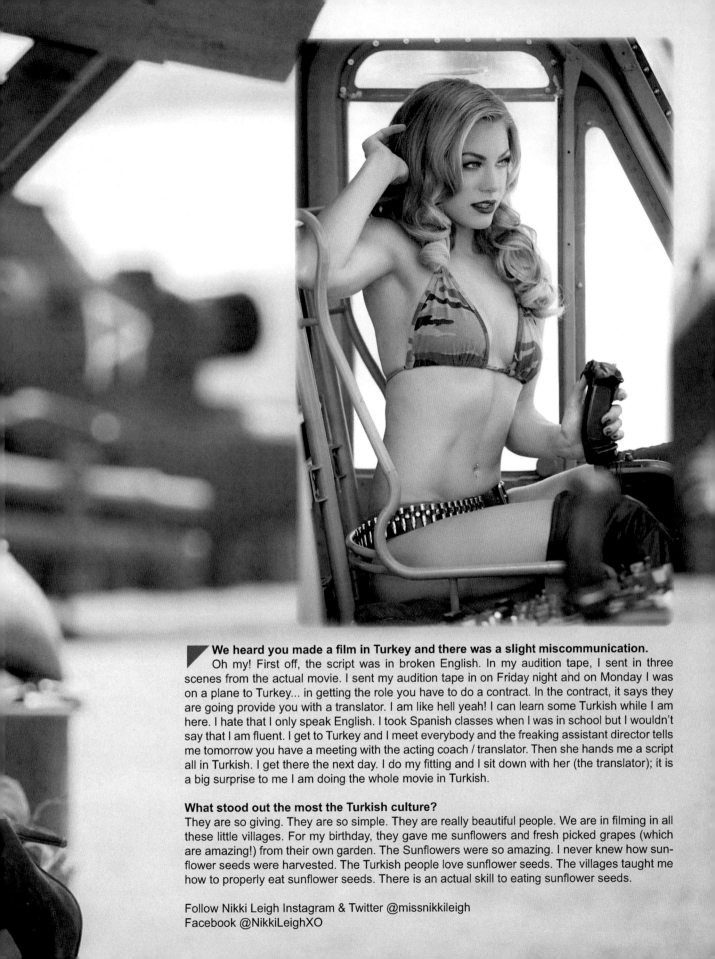

We heard you made a film in Turkey and there was a slight miscommunication.
Oh my! First off, the script was in broken English. In my audition tape, I sent in three scenes from the actual movie. I sent my audition tape in on Friday night and on Monday I was on a plane to Turkey... in getting the role you have to do a contract. In the contract, it says they are going provide you with a translator. I am like hell yeah! I can learn some Turkish while I am here. I hate that I only speak English. I took Spanish classes when I was in school but I wouldn't say that I am fluent. I get to Turkey and I meet everybody and the freaking assistant director tells me tomorrow you have a meeting with the acting coach / translator. Then she hands me a script all in Turkish. I get there the next day. I do my fitting and I sit down with her (the translator); it is a big surprise to me I am doing the whole movie in Turkish.

What stood out the most the Turkish culture?
They are so giving. They are so simple. They are really beautiful people. We are in filming in all these little villages. For my birthday, they gave me sunflowers and fresh picked grapes (which are amazing!) from their own garden. The Sunflowers were so amazing. I never knew how sunflower seeds were harvested. The Turkish people love sunflower seeds. The villages taught me how to properly eat sunflower seeds. There is an actual skill to eating sunflower seeds.

Follow Nikki Leigh Instagram & Twitter @missnikkileigh
Facebook @NikkiLeighXO

Kandy Magazine

KHLOE TERAE

"6 Year Anniversary Cover Model"

Khloe Talks Men

Photographer: Jenya Luzan @TropicPic
MUA: Edna Trogen @edna_trogen
Hair: Simona Barbato @simobarbato
Event: Destination Cover @destinationcover
PR: Nova Prime PR@novaprimepr
Wardrobe: Gigi The Label @gigithelabel | Montce Swim @montce_swim
Location: Oia Sunset Villas - Oia, Santorini, Greece @oiasunsetvillas

Her is nickname is KLO and her hidden talent is.. contortionist.
You don't find women like Khloe. They find you.

Khloe Talks Men

What is the first thing you notice about a guy? How tall he is.

What would be an immediate turn-off? Bad breath and bad attitude.

How far would you go on a first date? Depends on who it is.

What would you consider dirty-talk? I'm gonna come cook for you baby.

What does a man have to do to impress you? Don't slide into my DMs and be a typical douche-bag; be smarter than my generation.

What is the funniest pickup line a guy has used? I'd slide into more than just your DM's baby but that just came to mind because I received it this morning.

Have you ever been hit on by a woman? All the time, I'd say I get hit on by women just as much as men. It's flattering.

Do you recall your first kiss? I was in grade 7, he was in grade 8 and it was during the intermission of the show where he was the star. He was my boyfriend, we later went to prom together.

Follow Khloe Online
Instagram @khloe
Twitter @khloe
FB @khloeterae
khloeterae.ca

Kandy Magazine

Amanda Paris
9 Year Anniversary Cover Model

Photos Mike Prado
Hair and Makeup Adriana Marizcurrena

With over one and a half million fans on social media, Amanda Paris has become an one person marketing force. With curves in all the right places, Amanda has blanketed social media with her presence. Her Instagram page gives fans a peek at the life of a glamorous model. Over on her YouTube Channel, we get a look at her funny side. And, on TikTok, well isn't that all about being silly. So, remember to add Amanda to your social media following and enjoy these photos taken exclusively for Kandy magazine.

◢UNDER THE KANDY WRAPPER

Are you from a small town or the big city?
From a very small town.

Big sister, middle child or little sister?
Big Sister! I have 3 younger brothers.

Who was your 6th grade teacher?
Wow! Hmmm… man, I honestly can't remember. It was middle school to be fair though, so we had a different teacher for each subject.

Why did you move to LA?
More opportunities in the entertainment industry and better weather!!!

Tell us about your YouTube Channel.
I have a new series I'm working on that is going to be super fun, so you definitely don't want to miss that! You can also find some comedy sketches to make ya laugh or wild challenges. I also do a lot of fashion hails and vlogs.

Share some insight with our readers on the motivation behind these photos.
Look sexy AF. Lol. Honestly, we put our heads together with some of our favorite shots and found a way to recreate them with our own unique twist.

Describe Mr. Right in 3 words.
Loyal. Secure. Silly.

Any thoughts of moving back to Missouri?
Never! Lol. I love where I'm from, but I need something more fast paced. Plus, they aren't shooting many movies or tv shows in Missouri.

If you could raise a family anywhere in the world, where would that be?
Somewhere a lot cheaper than LA! Lol.

Follow Amanda
Instagram @MissAmandaParis
TikTok @MissAmandaParis
Facebook.com/MissAmandaParis
Twitter @MissAmandaParis
YouTube.com/AmandaParis

Look sexy AF..."

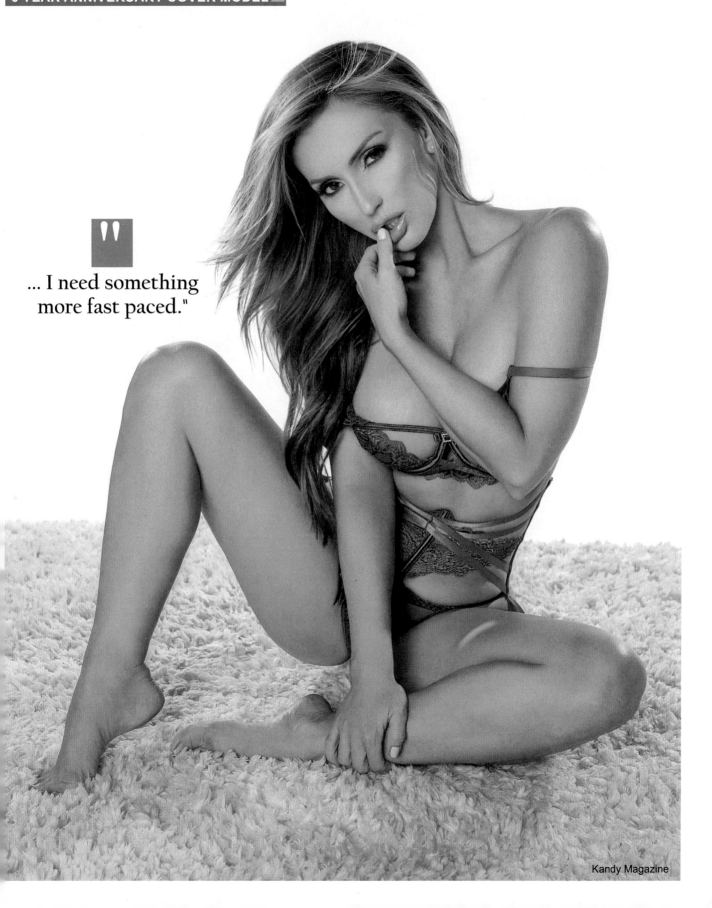

"

... I need something
more fast paced."

Jennifer Irene

"SHOOTING WITH THE STARS"

We say move aside "Dancing With The Stars."
It's time for an exciting competition show that appeals to real America.
"Shooting With The Stars" with host Jennifer Irene

Interview by Ron Kuchler
Photos by Charles "Chaz" Rodriguez
Hair and Makeup by Jennifer Irene

You can still be sexy and beautiful
and be a family woman."

Kandy Cover Model Jennifer Irene has worked with many Stars at Taran Tactical, where she is a tactical trainer.

Over the years, she has been fortunate to train with Keanu Reeves, Halle Berry, Josh Duhamel, The Kardashians, Post Malone, Joe Rogan, and Heidi Klum… to name a few Hollywood Stars.

KANDY: Hi Jen! Welcome back to Kandy. I realized it has been 7 to 8 years since you first appeared on the magazine cover of Kandy.
Jennifer Irene: Oh, my goodness. It was a long time ago. Those were really good years for me in the modeling world.

Educate us.
I was doing conventions; I was a spokesmodel for several companies. One of the best years I had in modeling. 12 to 13 covers including Maxim, FHM. I was on tour with VP Racing Fuels. I was a spokesmodel for them. I was traveling a lot, booking jobs internationally. I got to see cool parts of the world. I got to visit Asia. It was a very memorable year, especially being on the cover of Kandy.

What's your heritage again? There is some Asian blood I recall.
I am Fried Rice and Frijoles. Guess what that is.

What?
I am Taiwanese and Mexican.

I thought Filipino.
I look Filipino and I spent a lot of time in the Philippines in 2013 and 2014. I was traveling to the Philippines those summers. I was booking Women's Health Magazine, Shape Magazine, FHM, and Maxim. It was crazy. That was a fun year.

Fast forward to 2018. Mike Prado shoots you for the cover again. This time at the Kandy beach house. Red, White, and Blue theme.

That was definitely fun. It was fun to shoot at the Kandy beach house too.

Is this the first cover shoot since having a kid?
I did a cover for a shooting magazine and a couple other shooting magazines and also showed up on the cover of some other shooting magazine in France that I had no idea about. Somebody sent me a picture from the airport in France and I said, hey that's me. That's cool.

How was it to step back in front of the camera for a glamour shoot?
It was really nice. It was invigorating. I have been working really hard since having the baby to get my fitness back in check. It's easier said than done. It's a new life I have. I think it is inspiring to other women out there too who are afraid to embrace motherhood. You can still be sexy and beautiful and be a family woman. It was really nice.

We believe that you should embrace a woman's entire career, not just when she is starting in her 20s. And I think our readers appreciate witnessing the maturation of the models and celebrities who have appeared in Kandy over the years. Yes, definitely.

We follow your Instagram page dedicated to Firearms training. I would call it more Tactical Training. We work with a lot of influential people in entertainment, particularly for their roles in movies or self-defense. We had the Kardashians come out; we had a chance to work with Keanu Reeves and Halle Berry for John Wick. I got to do a couple yoga poses with Halle Berry. That was really cool. She was one of the nicest people I ever met.

Did you take a selfie with Halle?
I did. I pinned a few of them on my Instagram where I was doing yoga with Halle.

Let's talk Keanu.
Taran Tactical, Taran Butler is the owner of the company and also the main trainer. He has been working with Keanu for a while. Once in a while, he allows a few trainers to work alongside him and Keanu. I am one of them. Getting to work with Keanu has really been eye-opening to me. Not only is he humble and kind,

but he's also genuinely talented. That man went out there and he shredded. He was eager to learn and perfect his tactical skills. And I think that played a big role in making the movie so good. He did an amazing job. I have mad respect for him.

When guests are involved in Tactical Training and working with live bullets, are they wearing headsets to muffle the noise? Are the guns loud?
Everybody has to wear eye protection and ear protection when using any firearms on the tactical range. For people unfamiliar with guns we start them from basic. We don't go hot. Hot means a live bullet. We start with a laser. We work with them on form and go through gun safety. We have people come out all the time. Heidi Klum came out. Post Malone. We have people come out who are not familiar with guns and within two to three hours of training, they are shredding.

Was there a time when more people were inquiring?
During covid, when all the riots and chaos were taking place in our world, a lot more people were coming out of the woodwork and were interested in self-defense or inquiring about it. We were able to help a lot of people become familiar with the basics and in some cases change their viewpoints about guns and gun safety.
This was in 2020, correct? Yes.

In 2020, you said during covid. Was this Summer 2020 or Fall 2020?
Home invasion was on the rise; we had a few celebrities who had issues with intruders and were being robbed. They came out and wanted to learn about gun safety and which gun would be best for them in home protection. We were able to help them out at Taran Tactical, with what to do and how to point and shoot.

I saw Joe Rogan was out there.
Joe Rogan trains with us quite a bit a lot. I got to work with him. Taran Butler, the owner, is the main person and the main trainer. I am one of the few female trainers to work with Joe Rogan. I got to work with him 4 to 5 times. He is really nice..

Joe Rogan has a martial art, self-defense background with the UFC, etc... Why his interest in guns?
Why not. The more you learn, the more

you realize, the less you know.
That's true.
Even if you are not familiar with or are Pro-gun or if you are intimidated by guns, it would be beneficial to learn how to operate one. God forbid you are ever in a situation with a bad guy… you can see or know how to disarm them or know how to handle the gun or what to look out for … having the knowledge of how it works, helps you, helps your safety, and helps your security.

How does a woman such as yourself, who is a model and host, make her way into the world of tactical training?
I was shooting the cover of a magazine, and the owner of Stunt Players loaned me his car for the cover of the photo shoot. He introduced me to Taran Butler. My first day out there training was with Josh Duhamel. I was goo-goo, ga-ga. That was my first experience with Taran Tactical. He (Taran) believed in me and truly kind of took me under his wing and trained me from scratch. I was driving out to Simi Valley two to three times a week. Next thing you know I was in a shooting competition and now here I am with the company several years later. It was just a blessing in disguise.

What was your initial point of view going into this? Were you Pro 2nd Amendment?
I was definitely a beginner and Pro 2nd Amendment. My brother and sister are in the military. I have a lot of first responder friends. At the time, I was actually dating a cop. Definitely Pro 2nd Amendment. That was not an issue for me. I just wasn't familiar with shooting, and it took the proper training and proper knowledge of how to physically handle a gun and know how it works to feel secure and comfortable with and not so afraid of it.

You are on the way right now to the range. Yes. We have filming going on today. We have a YouTube celebrity coming out. Back in January, the second nicest person I met was Post Malone. He is so freaking cool. He is generally a kind-hearted person.

Follow Jen on Instagram
Tactical Training @jenniferireneshooter
Modeling @jenniferireneofficial

I am a sponsored athlete with 1st Phorm."

If you Google Jennifer Irene
Keanu Reeves Halle Berry
that video got more than
40 million views."

HOUSE OF DRAGON
Genre: Fantasy/Drama
Where: HBO
Episodes: 10

Storyline: Based on George R.R. Martin's "Fire & Blood," the House of Dragon series, set 200 years before the events of "Game of Thrones," tells the story of House Targaryen.

Photographs Courtesy of Ollie Upton / HBO

Unlike the Game of Thrones, where characters' maturations were in line with the actors portraying them, House of Dragon accelerates the maturity of two key characters, whereby requiring the replacement of the actors very early in the series. Milly Alcock, who portrays the Young Princess Rhaenyra, departs the series after episode 5. In future episodes, Emma D'Arcy portrays an older Princess Rhaenyra. Emma has large shoes to fill as Milly quickly made Princess Rhaenyra one of the most impressive television female characters this decade. We were ready to tell Beth from Yellowstone to move over. There is a new Queen Bitch on the throne. Then Dragon writers cast Milley onto the scrap heap. For shame, for shame; to borrow a line or word from the original Game of Thrones series.

The writers, in a short period of time, do establish a fierce rivalry for the heir to the throne, currently occupied by Princess Rhaenyra's father, King Viserys Targaryen (Paddy Considine) – who was chosen by the lords of Westeros to succeed the Old King, Jaehaerys Targaryen, at the Great Council at Harrenhal - and who is husband to Princess Rhaenyra's childhood best friend young Alicent Hightower (Emily Carey). Emily Carey is replaced in future episodes. Olivia Cooke assumes the role of Alicent Hightower, now Queen and mother to Aegon Targaryen, the first-born son of King Viserys.

In one of the early episodes of Dragon, upon the death of his wife, King Viserys names his daughter Princess Rhaenyra as the heir to the Iron Throne. She is of pure Valyrian blood, and she is a dragonrider. When Otto Hightower, the Hand of the King, decides the announcement of Princess Rhaenyra as the heir unacceptable, he manipulates the surroundings of the King to bring his daughter Alicent closer to the king, knowing that eventually the King will be pressured to take a new wife. The plan bears fruit when undue pressure from the king's council forces him to take a new wife. The king breaks his daughter's heart by choosing Alicent and Princess Rhaenyra's trust in Alicent.

When Alicent gives birth to Aegon Targaryen - it is said that whenever a Targaryen is born, the gods toss a coin in the air - the Hand and the council assume that Aegon will be the heir to the throne. King Viserys refutes these suggestions and restates that his first-born Princess Rhaenyra is the heir to the Iron Throne.

The battle for the Iron Throne is between Princess Rhaenyra, Alicent, and - did we forget to mention the king's brother - Prince Daemon Targaryen (Matt Smith), a dragonrider. Daemon possesses the true blood of the dragon.

Hidden in the shadows, we are keen to observe Princess Rhaenys Targaryen (Eve Best), a dragonrider herself, who has been providing counsel to Young Princess Rhaenyra. "The Queen Who Never Was" Princess Rhaenys was passed over as heir to the throne at the Great Council because the realm favored her cousin, Viserys, simply for being male.

In the realm of the House of Dragon, only one type of person may ascend to the Iron Throne, and that person must be a dragonrider.

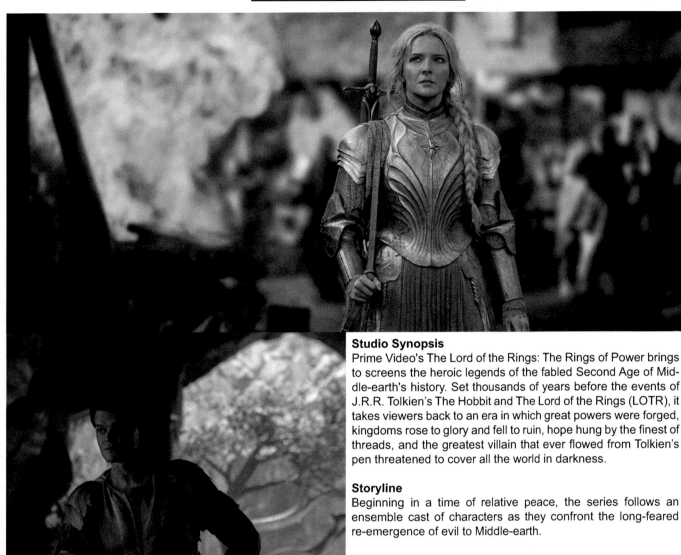

Studio Synopsis
Prime Video's The Lord of the Rings: The Rings of Power brings to screens the heroic legends of the fabled Second Age of Middle-earth's history. Set thousands of years before the events of J.R.R. Tolkien's The Hobbit and The Lord of the Rings (LOTR), it takes viewers back to an era in which great powers were forged, kingdoms rose to glory and fell to ruin, hope hung by the finest of threads, and the greatest villain that ever flowed from Tolkien's pen threatened to cover all the world in darkness.

Storyline
Beginning in a time of relative peace, the series follows an ensemble cast of characters as they confront the long-feared re-emergence of evil to Middle-earth.

Kandy 411
The kingdoms alluded to in the Studio Synopsis appear to center on Middle-earth's Southlands, the majestic forests of the elf-capital of Lindon, and the breathtaking island kingdom of Númenor. The most impressive characters thus far, in our eyes, are the elf warrior Galadriel and Queen Regent Míriel. Episodes are deep in character development. Perhaps necessary for the long-term viability of the series, but it is a heavy ball and chains dragging on-the-series attraction to viewers outside of LOTR fandom. In our opinion, the character development could have been equally attained with the usage of flashbacks, as HBO undertook in its' series 'Winning Time.'

Galadriel has established herself as the most intriguing character of the series. Her gut tells her Orcs are forming in the Southlands and is desperate to quell their assembly before becoming an overwhelming threat to Middle-earth. Unfortunately, she has no support from her fellow elves or man until Queen Regent is delivered a sign. We anticipate the remainder of season 1 to focus on an impending conflict between the Orcs and the men of the kingdom of Númenor.

The Lord of the Rings: The Rings of Power
Amazon Studios
Directors: J.A. Bayona, Wayne Che Yip, Charlotte Brändström
Key Characters: Galadriel (Morfydd Clark), Elrond (Robert Aramayo), Arondir (Ismael Cruz Córdova), Isildur (Maxim Baldry), Queen Regent Míriel (Cynthia Addai-Robinson), Theo (Tyroe Muhafidin), Halbrand (Charlie Vickers)
Photo credit: Ben Rothstein/Prime Video

ESCAPE FROM KABUL

Studio: HBO Documentary Films in association with the BBC, in collaboration with ARTE France, an AMOS Pictures Production
Genre: Documentary
Where: HBO
Directed by Jamie Roberts
Photographs Courtesy of HBO

Studio Says

ESCAPE FROM KABUL unfolds over 18 monumental days in August 2021, from the U.S. withdrawal of its troops from Afghanistan through the subsequent evacuation of tens of thousands of Afghan citizens from Kabul airport after the Taliban seized the city. This deeply immersive and emotional documentary combines never-before-seen archival footage from those on the ground at the airport, with exclusive interviews with people who were there throughout the period, including Afghan citizens attempting to flee, U.S. Marines tasked with managing the evacuation, and Taliban commanders and fighters who had recently taken the city. ESCAPE FROM KABUL is rooted in the unexpected and historic confrontation that occurred at Kabul airport and unfolds in dramatic moment-by-moment telling over two and a half pivotal weeks.

After 20 years of war between the Taliban, (an Islamic fundamentalist group) and NATO forces, a small force of U.S. Marines were deployed to Kabul on August 13 intending to evacuate U.S. citizens and "at risk" Afghans who had cooperated with the Americans and Allied Forces during the conflict. The orderly evacuation was meant to be implemented by the agreed-upon deadline of August 31, but when the Taliban unexpectedly took control of the city two days after the Marines arrived, plans changed.

Fearing reprisals and crackdowns on human rights from the Taliban, thousands of Afghan men, women, and children rushed to the airport, seeking an escape route. Taliban fighters, including suicide troops, encircled the airport perimeter in an uneasy truce with U.S. and Allied forces. With little advance planning, U.S. Marines battled daily to reclaim the overwhelmed airfield, all while a humanitarian catastrophe unfolded, with Afghan citizens spending days on end in the Kabul heat, without access to food or water, waiting to get through the gates to the airport. As the crowds grew increasingly desperate to leave, a tragic sequence of events unfolded, including a devastating suicide bomb attack that ISIS claimed responsibility for, killing 13 U.S. military personnel and more than 170 Afghan civilians.

Despite the chaos and suffering, 124,000 people were evacuated during the Kabul airlift, the largest in modern U.S. history, marking a devastating end to America's longest-running war. A final coda, filmed in spring of 2022, confirms the Taliban government's restrictions on women and girls and violent reprisals, leaving an uncertain future for many Afghan citizens who were not able to evacuate in August 2021.

Kandy Says

It's hard not to recall the horror playing out on our television and mobile devices screens those last few days of August 2021. This documentary shines a darker light on those days. If you were, as we were, horrified at the human tragedy unfolding in Afghanistan, prepare yourself to relive that horror and tremble at the utter incompetence of the Biden administration in ignoring the security and safety threats made crystal clear to them.

SUBSCRIBE TO PRINT EDITIONS
Make Checks Out to:
Kandy Enterprises LLC
7260 W. Azure Dr. Ste 140-639
Las Vegas, NV 89130
Yes! I want KANDY! SEND ME:

6 issues for $48 (1 Year) Only $8 per issue

12 issues for $84 (2 Years) Only $7 per issue

_____
First Name

_____
Last Name

_____
Street Address

_____
Street Address

_____
City

_____
State

_____
Zip Code

Payment Enclosed
Please allow 4 to 6 weeks for delivery of first issue.

For Credit card, Paypal and other payment options
go to https://kandy.store

PRINT 11 YEAR 2022

iPhone 14 Pro and 14 Pro Max

They come in the color Purple. Let us repeat that. They come in the color Purple, and you will be the envy of all the ladies in your life and who cross your path.

Powered by A16 Bionic - the fastest chip in a smartphone - the iPhone 14 Pro and iPhone 14 Pro Max represent the biggest technological leap ever for iPhone featuring the Dynamic Island, an e-SIM (goodbye SIM tray), the first-ever 48MP camera on iPhone, the Always-On display, and groundbreaking safety capabilities - Crash Detection, Emergency SOS via satellite

Details

Pricing: iPhone 14 Pro starts at $999, iPhone Pro Max Starts at $1,099

Colors: Deep purple, silver, gold, space black

Materials: Ceramic Shield front cover, surgical-grade stainless steel and textured matte glass

Sizes: 6.1-inch and 6.7-inch

Display: Always-On, Super Retina XDR display with ProMotion

Refresh Rate: 1Hz

SIM: eSim

Brightness: up to 2000 nits

Leather Wallet with MagSafe and Leather Cases: available in five new colors: midnight, forest green, ink, umber, and orange

Clear Case and Silicone Cases: available in midnight, storm blue, red, chalk pink, lilac, elderberry, succulent, and sunglow.

Take Me To The Island

Let's simply refer to it as The Island. All the pre-release propaganda focused on the camera system. And not to sell the camera system short as it is top notch. However, in our opinion, The Island is the star of this new iPhone. The annoying black notch of previous iPhone models is gone, replaced by The Island which resides under the glass. Depending on the activities, it automatically resizes vertically and horizontally to place those activities at the touch of a finger. The Island is unique and may take a few days to acclimatize to, resulting in you possibly missing a call or two; we speak from personal experience, of course. We're not ones to tout other publications but the Wall Street Journal has a great iPhone 14 Pro review video on their website wsj.com in which they highlight The Island.

Pro Camera System

Next up. iPhone 14 Pro introduces a new class of pro camera system, with the 48MP Main camera featuring a quad-pixel sensor, and Photonic Engine, an enhanced image pipeline that dramatically improves low-light photos. Creative professionals will love this camera system.

But, let's put this in perspective. There is a 99% likelihood that you are not a creative professional. You are not an Instagram model or TikTok(er). You are not a professional photographer nor do you work on a Hollywood set. You're an average Joe. This is still the iPhone and camera system for you. Why? It will

allow you to capture images up to 48 MB! Why is that important? For starters, it is billboard-size photography, not that you plan on taking out a billboard for your photography. But, let's bring it back to earth.

Do you get together for family portraits? Do you send out family Christmas cards with a photo of the entire family?

Do you attend concerts? Oops, scratch that. Bands and venues may not appreciate this shared knowledge. Do you attend live sporting events? Of course, we are talking amateur sports, not professional sports where they require a press permit to capture professional quality photographs.

Lastly, do you simply enjoy taking photos and wish you could blow them up and hang them on your walls? Now, you can do all this yourself. You no longer need to sit in front of a professional photographer for your annual family portrait as long as you are willing to take a few hours to learn the basics of lighting and aperture importance. In the long run, you will save hundreds, possibly thousands of dollars in professional photography fees.

Our One Last Thing - *eSIM set up*

▶ Apple says eSIM allows users to easily connect or quickly transfer their existing plans digitally and easily set up their device. While it may be a more secure alternative to a physical SIM card and allow for multiple cellular plans on a single device, our personal experience with eSIM was not easy or quick. Before we dive into the details, if you plan on trading in your old iPhone, we recommend holding onto that phone until you are certain you have transferred all the data off your old iPhone. We'll explain in a minute.

While setting up your new iPhone 14 Pro, Apple provides an option to use Bluetooth technology over a WiFi connection to transfer the data and information from your old iPhone (in our case, the iPhone X) to your new iPhone 14 Pro.

When the two phones are side by side, the iPhone 14 Pro will recognize your old iPhone and walk you through transferring data to your new iPhone. What happens if your iPhone 14 Pro inexplicably fails to recognize your old iPhone or something malfunctions connecting the two iPhones? This occurred to us. We were forced to connect to our iCloud account and download our backup to our new iPhone 14 Pro.

However, one small or shall we say big problem. We don't back up our old iPhone due to limited iCloud account size and to keep big brother out of our business. We had to go to our iPhone X and, in Settings, manually select which apps to back up to iCloud. Unless you are in a professional environment connected to a high-speed WiFi network, the upload time to back up a device could take hours, as it did in our case. Fortunately, most residential Internet plans provide faster download speeds, compared to their upload speeds. Downloading the data to our new iPhone 14 Pro was considerably faster than uploading our iPhone X.

Why should you hold onto your old iPhone? No matter how diligent you may be in backing up your data, there is a very high likelihood that some important data was not backed up and therefore not transferred. And the only way to ascertain is to have in your possession your old iPhone. We were alerted to this problem when we realized that we were not receiving existing new text messages of existing text message strings via Apple's iMessage feature on our new iPhone 14 Pro. They were routed to our old iPhone. As we dove deeper into the issue, we discovered that not all our text messages transferred to our new iPhone. After spending some time performing a web search for the reasons why we discovered the problem and were able to correct it.

With the inadvertent diversion of text messages resolved, we moved on to our next issue – missing apps and their logins. We have dozens of apps, installed with dozens of different login names and passwords. Of course, we rely on Apple's FACE ID to log into these apps. Who can recall all their login names and passwords? Unfortunately, many apps and/or their crucial login credentials did not transfer. As we go to press, we are still in the process of identifying missing apps and their missing login credentials.

Finally, the Photos app on your iPhone is likely the most extensive directory on your device. And if you have a limited iCloud account, you most likely do not backup Photos to your iCloud, the situation in our case. If these photos and videos are personally important, we recommend you upload to iCloud now.

Conclusion

▶ The iPhone 14 Pro and iPhone 14 Pro Max are the best iPhones ever. None of the previous models come close, not even the new basic iPhone 14, which really is not basic when compared to past iPhone models. Obviously, in these tough economic times amid a recession and record high inflation, it may be difficult to justify the steep expense on a mobile phone. But if your budget has the discretionary space, we highly recommend you execute the expenditure. In the US, many wireless companies are offering low monthly payment plans on these iPhones which would merely require one or two fewer Starbucks purchases per week. Certainly, you can reduce your Starbucks addiction to own a magnificent device.

Apple Watch Series 8

New features include Crash Detection for severe car crashes, international roaming, and watchOS 9

Price: Starts at $399 (US)
Available: Australia, Canada, France, Germany, India, Japan, UAE, UK, US, and more than 40 other countries and regions
Cases: Aluminum and stainless steel
Colors: Aluminum - starlight, midnight, silver, (PRODUCT) RED; Stainless steel - silver, graphite, gold
Sizes: 41mm and 45mm
Battery Life: 18-hour
Low Power Setting: disables or limits specific sensors and features, extends battery life up to 36 hours.
OS: watchOS 9
Perk: Three months of Apple Fitness+

Recommendation: If you are our typical Kandy reader and don't have plans anytime soon to be in a car accident, then we see little motivation for acquiring the Apple Watch 8. However, based on the features geared towards women (which we do not cover), it would make a nice gift for your wife, mother, sister or girlfriend. We intentionally did not mention mistress as you don't want to give her the wrong idea about her role in your life. If you don't own an Apple Watch and have been considering purchasing one in the past, you may want to consider the lower priced Apple Watch 8SE. And if you are an active outdoorist, we recommend reading our review inside this same issue of the Apple Watch Ultra.

Key New Features

Apple Watch 8 features a large, Always-On Retina display and a crack-resistant front crystal and all-day 18-hour battery life. It builds on its health and safety features like the ECG app and fall detection by introducing features specifically tailored towards women such as temperature-sensing capabilities and retrospective ovulation estimates. All sexes will benefit from the new crash detection and international roaming features.

Crash Detection: Leverages an advanced sensor-fusion algorithm and a new, more powerful accelerometer and gyroscope in Apple Watch to detect and deliver accurate car crash alerts,

Low Power Mode: extends battery life to 36 hours for Apple Watch Series 8 with iPhone present

watchOS 9 new features and enhanced experiences:
• New, more customizable watch faces - Lunar and Metropolitan
• International roaming
• FDA-cleared AFib History
• Redesigned Compass app
• Workout app:new in-session views, advanced workout experiences, new Multisport workout, and new running form metrics
• Sleep tracking introduces sleep stages
• New Medications experience inside the Health App

Crash Detection

When Apple Watch detects a severe car crash, the device will prompt you to check in and dial emergency services if there is no response after a 10-second countdown. Emergency responders receive the device location, which is also shared with your emergency contacts.

When Apple Watch and iPhone are present, Crash Detection works seamlessly to get help efficiently. When a severe car crash is detected, the emergency services call interface will appear on Apple Watch, as it is most likely to be in closer proximity, while the call is placed through iPhone if it is in range for the best possible connection.

Low Power Mode

This new mode temporarily disables or limits select sensors and features, including the Always-On Retina display, workout auto-start, heart health notifications, and others.

Medications Experience

Medications on Apple Watch and iPhone helps manage and track medications, vitamins, and supplements.

The new Medications experience enables the creation of a medications list, set up schedules and reminders, and view information on medications in the Health app.

Workout App

The new Workout app now includes Heart Rate Zones to help users improve fitness.

• The Workout app includes new in-session views, such as Segments, Splits, and Elevation, that offer more precise workout data.

• Improve training with advanced workout experiences, including Heart Rate Zones, Custom Workouts, Pacer, and, coming later this year, Race Route.

• For triathlons or activities with any sequence of swimming, biking, or running, the new Multisport workout uses autodetection to easily switch between workouts and records transition times.

• New running form metrics, including Stride Length, Ground Contact Time, and Vertical Oscillation, can all be added as metrics on Workout Views.

Sleep Tracking

Sleep tracking in watchOS 9 adds sleep stages, a new feature that uses signals from the accelerometer and heart rate sensor to estimate REM, Core, or Deep sleep.

• Apple Watch uses signals from the accelerometer and heart rate sensor to estimate when you are in REM, Core, or Deep sleep.

• Sleep stage data viewed directly on Apple Watch in Sleep app

• More detailed information is found in the Health app on iPhone, including interactive sleep stages charts, time asleep, heart rate or respiratory rate, in sleep comparison charts.

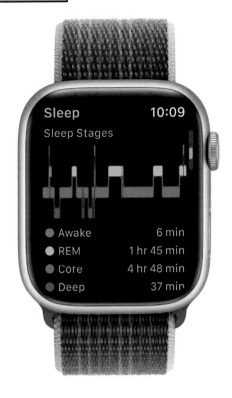

Compass App

The redesigned Compass app provides more in-depth information and new zoomable views. The app displays a new hybrid view that simultaneously shows both an analog compass dial and a digital view. Turning the Digital Crown reveals an additional view that includes latitude, longitude, elevation, and incline

New Bands and New Faces

With Apple Watch Studio, Apple Watch Series 8 can be paired with any available band in the same collection. Apple Watch Nike and Apple Watch Hermès debut new bands and watch faces this fall. Nike has vibrant new Sport Band colors and a new Sport Loop with the "Just Do It" logo woven into the band.

Starting this fall, any Apple Watch user running watchOS 9 — even those without a Nike model — will be able to access all the Nike watch faces, including the fresh colors coming to the Bounce face.

Apple Watch Hermès

Apple Watch Hermès introduces two new bands: H Diagonal, which creates a sporty pattern of the Hermès H with hundreds of microperforations, and Gourmette Metal, which features a polished stainless-steel chain and noir leather wrapping twice around the wrist.

A whimsical new Hermès watch face called Lucky Horse beautifully complements the new bands and celebrates the equestrian roots of the house with an animated horse that sleeps when the wrist is down and comes alive when it is raised.

Apple Watch Ultra
Built for Kandy readers who live life on the edge

The Apple Watch Ultra features a new bold design and a wide range of elements built for endurance, exploration, and adventure. It introduces a 49mm titanium case and flat sapphire front crystal resulting in the biggest and brightest Apple Watch display yet. A customizable Action button offers instant access to a wide range of features. The new Wayfinder watch face is designed specifically for the larger Apple Watch Ultra display and includes a compass built into the dial, with space for up to eight complications.

Details
Price: $799 (US)

Battery Life: During normal use, up to 36 hours of battery life with iPhone present.

Low-power Setting: ideal for multi-day experiences, can extend battery life to reach up to 60 hours.

Water Resistance Rating: 100 meters under ISO standard 22810.

Wrist Bands: Three new bands — Trail Loop, Alpine Loop, Ocean Band.

OS: watchOS 9 which requires iPhone 8 or later and iPhone SE (2nd generation) or later running iOS 16

Perk: Three months of Apple Fitness+ are included for customers

Recommendation: If you are an extreme athlete or an avid outdoor enthusiast, it may be worth parting with the eight hundred bills to own. However, if your are neither of the above, you may wish to consider one the less expensive watches in the Apple Watch series.

Designed for water sports, including extreme activities like kitesurfing and wakeboarding, along with recreational scuba diving to 40 meters with the new Oceanic+ app, the Apple Watch Ultra is a must-own dive accessory.

With its WR100 certification, the watch is tested to survive extreme underwater adventures. The watch is also certified to EN 13319, which is an internationally recognized standard for dive accessories, including depth gauges that are relied upon by recreational divers around the world.

Utilizing a new depth gauge, it features a Depth app designed with an intuitive user interface. With just a glance, the Depth app displays time, current depth, water temperature, duration under water, and max depth reached. Divers can program the Action button to instantly launch the Depth app.

The new Oceanic+ app turns Apple Watch Ultra into a capable dive computer. Available from the App Store later this fall, the app runs the Bühlmann decompression algorithm, and includes dive planning, easy-to-read dive metrics, visual and haptic alerts, no-decompression limit, ascent rate, and safety stop guidance. Oceanic+ also offers a personalized user profile, reports on current and local dive conditions, and a dive logbook that can be shared with family and friends and automatically syncs to iPhone.

New Bands Designed for the Great Outdoors

Designed specifically for endurance athletes and runners, the Trail Loop band is the thinnest Apple Watch band to date. The lightweight woven textile is soft and flexible, allowing it to cinch to the optimal fit, and the convenient tab is designed for quick and easy adjustment.

Cave explorers and alike will enjoy the Alpine Loop band, featuring two integrated layers made from one continuous weaving process that eliminates the need for stitching. The top loops, interspersed with high-strength yarn, provide adjustability and a secure attachment for the titanium G-hook fastener.

The Ocean Band is built specifically for extreme water sports and recreational diving with a titanium buckle and corresponding spring-loaded loop. Molded from a flexible high-performance polymer designed for harsh conditions, it stretches and utilizes the tubular geometry for a secure fit. The Ocean Band also has an optional extra-long tail that allows users to comfortably wear over a wetsuit.

Bigger, Brighter, and Stronger

Made from aerospace-grade titanium, the watch balances weight, durability, and corrosion resistance. The case rises up to surround all edges of the flat sapphire front crystal, protecting the Retina display, which is up to 2000 nits — 2x brighter than any prior Apple Watch. The new Action button in high-contrast international orange is easily customized for instant access to a variety of features, including Workouts, Compass Waypoints, Backtrack, and more.

The watch has three built-in microphones to significantly improve voice calls sound quality during any conditions. An adaptive beamforming algorithm uses the microphones to capture voice while reducing ambient background sounds, resulting in remarkable clarity. In challenging windy environments, it uses advanced wind noise-reduction algorithms, including machine learning, to deliver clear and intelligible audio for calls.

Explorers

With the bigger, brighter display and rugged design, adventurers and explorers will appreciate the Apple Watch Ultra in a range of environments, whether daily commute adventures or extreme rock climbing in Yosemite.

The completely redesigned Compass app in watchOS 9 surfaces more in-depth information and three distinct views. The app displays a new hybrid view that simultaneously shows both an analog compass dial and a digital view. Turning the Digital Crown reveals an additional view that includes latitude, longitude, elevation, and incline, as well as an orienteering view showing Compass Waypoints and Backtrack.

Apple Watch SE

The redesigned Apple Watch SE delivers the core Apple Watch experience at a new starting price

Price: Starts at $249 (US)

Sizes: 40mm and 44mm

Colors: Midnight, Starlight, Silver finishes

Bands: Compatible with all bands

OS: watchOS 9

Perk: Three months of Apple Fitness+

Core Experience: Activity tracking, high and low heart rate notifications, and Emergency SOS, as well as the new Crash Detection feature

Recommendation: In these days of hyperinflation, the Apple Watch SE is a practical entry smartwatch for anyone on a budget, college students, or as a gift to a family member. We recommend the Apple Watch SE for these reasons.

Aluminum Back + S8 SiP dual-core processor

Apple Watch SE maintains the same case design but features a redesigned matching back case made of a nylon composite material, making it lighter than ever and perfectly matches the three classic case finishes.

Powerful upgrades include the S8 SiP advanced dual-core processor, the same processor that is in Apple Watch Series 8 and Apple Watch Ultra, making it 20 percent faster than the previous generation, along with international roaming.

Fun for the Whole Family

With Family Setup, family members who don't have their own iPhone can enjoy the features and benefits of Apple Watch. The new Apple Watch SE delivers advanced features at a low price and is a great way to enter the smartwatch realm, as well as a practical gift for family members.

Powered by watchOS 9, the new Apple Watch SE features more customizable watch faces, an enhanced Workout app, and the new Compass app, enhanced fitness and wellness features.

AirPods Pro (2nd generation)
the next generation of AirPods Pro

The new AirPods Pro produces its best audio quality to date, cancelling up to twice as much noise over its predecessor via enhanced Active Noise Cancellation, a new additional extra small ear tip, and a battery life up to 25% longer.

Details
Price: $249

Battery Life: up to 6 hours with Active Noise Cancellation, up to 30 hours of total listening time with Active Noise Cancellation by utilizing the case for four additional charges

Kandy Verdict: We have not jumped on the ear pods bandwagon yet. At a price of $249, we are definitely not there. We'll keep shuffling along with our trusty ear buds.

Highlights
With the power of the new H2 chip, the new AirPods Pro introduce break-through audio performance — including major upgrades to Active Noise Cancellation, and Transparency mode — while also offering a unique way to experience Spatial Audio that's even more immersive.

- enjoy Touch control for media playback
- adjust volume directly from the stem, a simple swipe up or down enables quick volume adjustments on the go
- enjoy a longer battery life, 1.5 hours longer than the 1st generation
- a brand-new charging case may be utilized four times before requiring a recharge itself, extending battery life up to 30 hours
- an additional new small ear tip size for a better fit

The H2 Chip
The H2 chip cancels up to twice as much noise over the previous generation. Plus, with a new low-distortion audio driver and custom amplifier, the AirPods Pro now offers richer bass and crystal-clear sound across a wider range of frequencies. Transparency mode makes it possible to stay connected to and aware of the world around you. Its Adaptive Transparency takes this feature even further. The powerful H2 chip enables on-device processing, which reduces loud environmental noise — like a passing vehicle siren, construction tools, or even loudspeakers at a concert — for more pleasant everyday listening.

XS Ear Tip
Since the best audio experience isn't complete without a great in-ear fit, a new extra small ear tip is included so even a wider range of people can enjoy AirPods Pro.

Personalized Spatial Audio
Personalized Spatial Audio enables a more immersive listening experience AirPods. Based on the size and shape of your head and ears, sound is perceived individually. Using the TrueDepth camera on your iPhone, you can create a personal profile for Spatial Audio that delivers a listening experience precisely tuned for you. The gamut of Personalized Spatial Audio enjoyment covers music, movies, and TV shows — with dynamic head tracking — across iPhone, iPad, Mac, and Apple TV.

Multiple Charging Options
Travelers – business or leisure – can now charge their AirPods Pro with an Apple Watch charger, in addition to a MagSafe charger, Qi-certified charging mat, or the Lightning cable. In addition, AirPods Pro come with a newly designed charging case that is sweat / water-resistant, and includes a lanyard loop. The charging case also has a built-in speaker to deliver louder tones.

A new low-distortion audio driver and custom amplifier offer richer bass and crystal-clear sound, while a new extra small ear tip delivers an even better fit.

TAWNY JORDAN

"7 Year Anniversary Cover Model"

Photos Tony Piazza

" ... I feel like I'll be telling my grandkids about it one day."

UNDER THE KANDY WRAPPER

From Kandy Krush of the Month to Kandy cover girl, you've joined a very rare club, Kandy girls who hold both titles. How does it feel?

From Kandy Krush of the Month to Kandy Cover Girl, I'm so flattered and thankful! When I was a little girl I always thought modeling would be amazing, but never thought I could achieve as much as I have. Thank you guys.

What was it like as a Ring girl on the Mayweather vs McGregor fight?

To be a part of the Mayweather vs McGregor fight was a once in a lifetime thing. I feel like I'll be telling my grandkids about it one day. I've been a ring girl for Corona Boxing for about 5 years and this was the biggest fight in history to date. I couldn't help but smile and feel the energy from the crowds from this hyped up fight!

What was your impression the fighters?

I have respect for both fighters, they are extremely talented and hard workers. It's amazing to see how these athletes train and perform, it's actually kind of inspiring to me because I love to box.

For the Kandy readers who are not avid Tawny followers, until now, please recall for them the Ibiza wave incident.

Haha oh goodness! So I was in Ibiza for an event and filming for an interview. For the interview I stood in an area with lots of water and the tide would come and go. As I was speaking into the mic I felt the cord pull and the water brush against my legs getting stronger and stronger, before you know it the tide swooped me off my feet and I tried not to get the mic wet. Everything was caught on the camera and definitely made it to the media. I'm ok though and the film crew came to my rescue, not sure if the mic made it though.

Final question, what would you say has been the biggest life changing moment since you started modeling?

The most pivotal moment in my career was when a model manager signed me to her agency. We worked together for about 6 years before she passed away. In those six years she helped shape me into who I am today, a model and a business woman. Never forget your roots.

Follow Tawny Instagram @TawnyJordan

Made in the USA
Las Vegas, NV
15 December 2023

82881948R00031